FOR THE STARGAZERS

THE DREAMERS

THE ROMANTICS

THE FANTASTS

When you ask me, "Which star is ours?"

I say, "All of them."

I have not been time traveling;
I have been traveling through time.

At night I close my eyes & dissipate into cloud atlas,
band & billow noctilucent, then rearrange in rare pattern.

*What a beautiful way to break apart.*

A letter to my love, who must be lost at sea.

Were most of your stars out? You forgot how to read charts.
You circumnavigate the earth searching for a compass that
works.
On land there is a woman made entirely of ocean. Her heart is
a storm.
It beats against the metal hull of her ribs, r e l e n t l e s s.

You think of her often.

Were most of your stars out? The constellations are crooked.
Planets no longer align properly. We are not magnetic.

I'm running out of ways to explain what you mean to me.

> You're gravity.
> You're the sun.
> You're the center of the universe.
> *Shut up.*

Were most of your stars out? In love we become nocturnal,
taciturn, we let our hands do all the talking, capsize
every night in a sea of bed sheets, reaching for a body
of water to drown in.          *You are not him.*

We will find each other as soon as our eyes adjust.

Were most of your stars out? Yes.
> every.single.one.

I. **FULL**

you are not
lost;
you are in
transit.

and the riptides
you fear
will take
your life
are the
currents
carrying you
into mine.

i.    This morning E. E. Cummings broke into your
home & stole your beloved typing machine.
The keys got stuck. Your brain stopped working.
Line        breaks     are another way to
                frac-
                      ture the soul.

ii.    When the Cole Bros. brought circus
carneys to Cape May they came with
               a heat wave
               shimmering gasoline vapor
               elephant dung
& a man named Charlie
        whose eyes befriended my big cat tattoo
        while my own rode

           the s p i n n i n g
           carousel
           of   his   black   teeth.

iii.    There are 7 billion people on this planet
& they are all made of
               tree       rings.

## PURPLE AVENS & PRAIRIE SMOKE

There used to be meadows in our chests.
We would walk among them pointing out
the purple avens & prairie smoke,
which are actually one & the same,
but we weren't botanists back then.

We'd roll around fields of nodding flowers,
nod off ourselves in tangled stems
until dreamscapes broke into delicate
red petals hiding beneath our eyelids.

In those days we made love from concentrate
& it was the sweetest thing you could ever taste.

## LOVE & LUNACY

In 360 B.C.E. Plato wrote, "Love is a madness."
Modern science has since validated this claim
with studies that show similarities occurring
in brain events involving love & lunacy.

Our romance is a chemical dance between
dopamine, adrenaline, & serotonin.

So when I tell you that every time I
> smell sandalwood on your skin
> hear your name from another's lips
> feel your breath on my neck
> see your face, I'm a wreck

because my brain lights up like a city at dusk,
my veins all flood, the planets rust.

& when I say I'm crazy,
deranged, lovesick & struck,
I'm not just making this up.

My dear, these are all symptoms
of the madness that is love.

## SMALL STEPS, GIANT LEAPS

What are the lies you tell yourself?

That it's impossible, will never work,
the pressure is far too much?

That the space between us is galaxies
we travel light-years just to touch?

How quickly you forget
we are astronauts.

Our small steps
are giant leaps.

Just you wait & see.

i.    The night you fell to your knees & whispered
mythologies into the canyon curve of my hips,
you were not careful. For days they echoed,
carbon-steel pinballs bouncing around tender
ligaments & bruising ribs. I have not
caught      my breath     since.

ii.    Recall how the sky appeared a smeared black-
board of promises you never intended to keep.
Bloodworms flooded from the earth, floundering
en masse unimaginable, ammonia-soaked. Stars

d    i s    s    o l    v e    d

in a chalk dust clap of applause for feats
that meant nothing. At least not to me.

iii.    We kept dried organs in canopic jars, un-
peeled dusty strips of linen, wrapped
hollow torsos in white gauze.

iv.    In time we will become archetypes. Linguists
will invent new words to describe the un-
precedented ways in which we hurt.

## SPACESHIPS

Tell me about the summer
you shed your fingerprints
& wrapped your palms
in heart lines, tied them
to the stars & swung.


Tell me how the moon
kissed your feet nude,
about how our bodies
became spaceships
by evening & blasted off
the heat of asphalt.


Tell me you miss those
shimmering nights
guided by sky maps
measuring the distance
between our lips.


*I do.*

Many nights passed
in that fashion,
bodies & lights
wet with neon,
blurred & abstract.
Much like a futurist
painting,
we moved
too fast.

## POP ROCKS & SODA POP

We were electric that night
the power lines collapsed
& you laughed because
our cell phones died
& I, for the life of me,
could not find a flashlight.
There were plenty of candles,
not a single match, &
only the palest moonlight
catching your skin
through open windows
as we listened to the winds howl
        the thunder clap
        the sky break
        the branches snap
& we explored the storms
that have long since existed,
braved the blizzards within,
traded breaths & tangled limbs,
all of this until the winds calmed
        the thunder died
        the sky healed
        the branches sighed
& we collapsed like power lines
because we were electric that night.

Speak to me in violets & vagueries
like you have a masterpiece
buried in the roots of your teeth
begging for extracting.

Touch me with white pepper palms
& fingers that move gingerly
across my skin like it's canvas
for words you haven't yet written.

& when you grip my whalebone hips
like rocks jutting into the Atlantic
    & when your knuckles turn white
    with odes not meant for the ocean
       & when the sky dims to witness
       fireworks burst from your mind

know that the show is not over—

that no moonbeam or starlight
or chemical cocktail finale
compares to basking in the
limelight glow of your eyes.

## STARGAZING

I wasn't admiring
the freckles on your skin;
I was stargazing.
& when I said I wanted
to make love to you,
I meant all of you.
& when you felt my fingers
tracing poetry
over parts of you that
were supposedly broken,
know that all I saw
were prisms, refracted light,
& everything I wanted
to make mine.

there is **is** no greater

wilderness

than a body

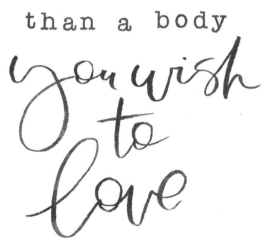

you wish
to
love

# BOTTLE ROCKETS

How can I regret
nights spent
shooting stars
like bottle rockets

we were comet tails
& tattered sails

we haven't
loved like that
since.

# THE EINSTEIN-ROSEN BRIDGE

i.    This is me in the past
                scolding you in the future
    for hanging hopes from vaulted ceilings,
    watching them dangle limp like so many

    d       a           s      a      s.
       e      d         t      r

    This is me on the back porch
                barely listening
    to the Tree Frog Symphony Orchestra
    play in E major while we talk about
             minor ironies.

ii.    Practicing paradiddles, s k i p p i n g stones,
    measuring distance with one eye [closed],
    staring down the throat of a black hole.

iii.    If there is a bridge that connects your universe
    & mine, you better believe I will find it.

iv.    The Perseids fly on mobiles,
    astronomical fevers burning up
    & breaking into cold sweats.

    We count red flags & white flares,
    daydream what it would be like to sleep.

## THE BRIGHTEST THING

I need you to know something—
that when you're feeling defeated
                beat up & down
                on your luck
when you feel like you haven't done
anything or enough
that the most important things in life
cannot be built with your hands.

& even on days you feel burnt out
                        dim in the darkness
                        lacking sheen

I need you to know—

you're still the
brightest damn thing
I've ever seen.

i.  Three nights ago I dreamt we were redwoods,
    majestic & towering, in a wilderness dense
    with metaphors that coalesced in fog mist.
    Our love had grown slow like an old forest,
    names carved in heartwood, layers of bark
    thick as thieves protecting unnumbered
    invisible cities contained within your
    skyscraper trunk.

ii. I took the stairs down instead of up.

iii. There will be others, I know. They will
    come & admire the texture of your skin,
    your august boughs, hacking off pieces
    to bring home, leaving you exposed,
    soft & fibrous, red-brown,
    fleshly.

iv. Our limbs may never touch, but roots
    laid shallow & wide will tangle beneath
    the earth. Of this, I am certain.

v.  When I awoke the trees fell in my chest.
    I was left, wondering if a dream
    is all we'd ever be.

## WILD THING

It is not a stretch to say
your eyes are satellites,
drawing everything in
with cosmic light
& sparkling curiosity.

Last night you were
the littlest cowboy,
lassoing fireflies
& kicking up stardust
wherever you jumped.

This morning you were
the tiniest lion man,
flipping your golden mane
from side to side
& roaring with delight.

Tomorrow you will be
no small wonder,
a wild thing stomping
footprints into the heart
of anyone who is watching.

I'm on the train to Killarney
shuffling through songs
when your voice comes on
thick with accent.
I can't see your face,
so I keep staring
at the Irish countryside,
details lost in a Monet
blur of greens that
pop against gray skies,
forehead against cold pane
fogging up from lips
too close to the window,

now shower steam,
flag falling
like a towel
around your feet.

## SANDSTORMS & MONSOONS

I don't know your laugh
or the sandstorms that
rage when you're mad,
escaping dust-filled lungs
in dry, tired gasps. But,

I know the way my name sounds
coming out of your mouth
at unearthly hours,
                    humid,
wet with monsoon,
                    heavy,
breathing that leaves me
breathless. & I know, I know,
more than anything, I know,
the stars shudder like our skin
across immeasurable distance
as we bury our needs

in each other.

Your engine caught fire
on I-95, exactly 30
miles from home.
I know
because I'd been
counting mile markers.
I do that sometimes
when there is just
no sense in
talking to you.
The rain was a
swirling mist & when
you got out of the car
you were a bear,
arms high above your
head, roaring that

if only it were
raining harder
we wouldn't be in
this mess.

That is always
your logic—
blame the rain.
You, love, are
without fault,
arms above your
head & all.

But if you're going to
lose your mind today,
then I will lose it
with you.

# THE RIFT

I did not notice the rift.

It went something like this:
one morning I awoke
to find an unknown
body of water between us.
Suddenly we were
separate continents

& I did not notice the rift.

# I'M SORRY, OKAY?

I'm sorry for bodies I explored
& lips I kissed that were not yours.

I'm sorry I don't know how to unlove or unfuck
former flames, even more so for the embers still aglow.

I'm sorry I can't extinguish every thought
that did not begin or end with how my curves
fit into your contours.

Mostly I'm sorry for running out of promises
I haven't already made before. But know this—

all the love I can't swear,
I will show.

## II. GIBBOUS

maybe it wasn't
a sign

*maybe the stars*
never aligned
but
*goddamnit*
isn't it so
*beautiful*
*to believe*
they did ?

Five months ago you sent a letter, & every day for the last five months I've checked the mailbox hoping it would come. Today, it finally came. Today, I stopped wondering what your air hand would say in its chicken-scratch calligraphy. I stopped imagining what your cologne would smell like, or if, after all this time, it would bring grapefruit apologies, peppermint remorse, & finish off by asking for deep cedar forgiveness. Today, I sat in my car with a swatch of red fabric from an old favorite sweater, soaked in the scent of you, closed my eyes & let the ocean tide pull of your soul bring me backward in time to five months ago. Five months ago, when there was no question that we were destiny, when nothing could come between what was always meant to be. My eyelids, overwhelmed by the swelling sea, could not keep their levee. Thoughts distended into daydreams, poetry you wrote about waking up hungover like swollen rain clouds & visiting our favorite coffee shop we don't even know the name of yet. Reveling in silence, faces so close our noses touch, only breaking it when one of us finds something important enough to say. Today, I finally let go of the pain I've been harboring, finally got closure from that moment, five months ago, when the universe fell asleep at the wheel.

## LONG DAYS, MEANINGLESS NIGHTS

Long days, meaningless nights.
The tides come & go, come & go.
Mostly, they just go, leave me
standing on a starless beach
alone,
          gazing into gunmetal seas
searching for the glint & glimmer
of hope.
          & the only thing I know
is how far I am from the woman
I want to become, the kind

who doesn't come undone
when the waves get rough,

the kind who doesn't sink
every time she lifts you up.

## CHARIOT THUNDER

There's a man inside of you
who you're aching to become,
whose bones grow faster
than the skin they're in.
A man whose muscles stretch
under the drumhead pressure
to exist, whose heart beats
in chariot thunder across
white marbled halls

while life,
the great sculptor,
chips away at them.

# YOU HUNG YOUR HEAD; I HELD MY TONGUE

That day you coughed
curses into the earth
             covered your mouth
             with dirt-caked palms
saw your brown eyes
in mine (for the first time).

That day two F-16s
flew overhead, unseen
                 pulling smoke
                 from your lungs
in contrails.

You hung your head;
I held my tongue.

That day you finally
recognized my sorrow—
an abandoned house
with boarded windows,
derelict & dying,
                 a tomb
not even a squatter
would occupy.

# A VICTOR, A VECTOR

To raise a good man, you must
begin by teaching him how to count.

But you jump from two to ten,
start laughing, devilish, clapping
all the beats you missed
like you've broken some
numeric law, found a wormhole,
traveled through space & time,
come out on the other side
a victor    a vector    a vivisection
of untamed animal.

Be patient, little one.
You have plenty of time
to race clocks,

but I
don't have enough
to slow them down.

## LOVE YOU BETTER

Let me find you
      rougher.

Let me find ink
      washed out & weathered
      mementos you carried
      for a man who is not you
      from a time that is not now.

Let me find skin
      well-worn & leathered
      on hands calloused
      by good intention
      but rugged with regret.

Let me find nothing
      left of women who
      loved you younger
      as I tend to wounds
      they failed to dress.

Let me find you
      rougher,
      love you better.

Remember yesterday when you
swore you wouldn't make it through
when you were buckled knees
                    & clenched teeth
when you wanted to fold up
into white flags dragging
from your feet

& you wondered
"where did all the magic go?"
so I told you

remember yesterday when you
swore you wouldn't make it through

you woke up this morning
didn't you?

# WOUNDS LIKE MINE

How can you not be here,
while every motorcycle for miles
coughs your name in exhaust,
while everything,
every damn thing,
is drenched in White Diamonds?
Come back to me
the way the minute hand
always comes back to the hour.
We'll let this clock unwind.

Whoever said time heals all wounds
did not have wounds like mine.

i.  Stop asking rhetorical questions.
        "Are you okay?"
                "I'm not okay."

ii. Thank you for wearing snowshoes. Be careful
    where you step, the    ice    is    breaking    up.
    Fall in & you won't survive more than 30 minutes.
    That's only if you can keep your head
                                    above
                                    water.
    That's only if angels decide to save you.
    (Spoiler: you're not the saving kind.)

iii. These are the glaciers that carved canyons
     in my heart. These are the auger-dug holes,
     the new cerulean calm waiting for something
     to come.

iv. Do you know what her brain looked like before
    the lobotomy? Like a city at night,
                    like northern lights.
    God,
            she fucking glowed in the dark.

## STARGAZING AT NOON

At the far side of the yard
my father is coughing sawdust
from his lungs again.

One day
you're so
close
I feel you
in my bones.

the next you're

farther

than the sun

# WILTING SUNS

"My favorite thing is the way he looks at you."

I am listening to you make beautiful things out of the dust.
Lowering octaves, humming on the fringe of something.

Like mahogany.
Like paperbark & tree stumps.
Like wilting suns.

Voices warm the floorboards.
   Stars twinkle acoustic.

You are always speaking honey & agave.
Dried mangos & magnolia. Lightning bugs.

We sing in cathartic harmony,
cardiac beats & flatline drums.

Just when I thought I couldn't read
the warning signs, flashing tail lights,
he jumped out of his Jeep,
approached my car, motioned
      for me to roll
      the window down
& kissed me hard.

& it felt like February
& it was fine in the fifties sense
& I realized how foolish we'd been

to believe we could keep mapping
the terrain of each other's bodies
without writing our own names
    proper like our favorite places
      (as if we weren't pioneers
      or the first to find God here).

So I folded up my love, stuffed it
in the glove compartment,
& drove away.

# I WANT, I WANT, I WANT

I want

> you underneath me
> like a bed of leaves
>
> above me
> like a canopy.

I want

> to explore every inch
>
> from your lashes
> to your limbs.

I want

> your breath
> so hot on my neck
>
> my skin catches fire.

& on the seventh day we don't rest
because how in God's name can you rest
when every breath is a beckoning

"Take me."

So we wake & whiskey
& we make love

like we make coffee—
sugary, extra sweet.

That is what Sundays are made of.

By the afternoon
you've had so much caffeine
you swear you can hear electricity.

We speak in frequencies.

The sheets are humming.

Our bodies are live wires.

# CERULEAN

*Cerulean.* Say it again. *Ce-ru-le-an.* Feel your breath
swell up out of your lungs, spill over your tongue in a soft,
foam-bright wind, hum & roll with a coo, u n d u l a t e,
then spread & flatten before gently crashing into the gums
behind your two front teeth. *This is not a siren song.*

Sing along
while you peel pages from the Julian calendar
          watch them fall like apples & angels.

"We don't need dates anymore," you explained.

The beaches have all turned to deserts,
          bodies to salt. It is the dead of winter.
We cling to what is obsolete, like apricity,
          like forgotten planets—a cold dead place.

"When we met Mercury was in retrograde & I could
smell Rome burning from six thousand miles away."

*Ave, Caesar, morituri te salutant.*

Charcoal. A smoke-stacked sky raining alphabets.
They seeped through my clothes. When I was done
taking notes, even my bones were soaked in poetry.

Rain tap dancing on a tin roof,
the rusty staccato of toe and heel,
a weathervane stuck on West—

who needs prediction
when you are the prevailing wind,
the constant, neither light,
nor variable, a migratory bird
                who comes back

year. after year. after year.

We stare at the horizon
& wait for the future
to arrive.

We reach for the sun,
as if our hands could hold fire,
as if it were a copper coin

& the night,
a bottomless well.

*I wish.*

## EMPIRES

I watch

      empires rise & fall in your chest
      the sun set in the east & rise in the west

&

I want

      to describe the way I feel this morning
      but the only word I can find is crumbling.

# LIKE RAIN ON WARM PAVEMENT

Speak to me in Italian.
>  *Voglio fare l'amore con te.*
What did you say?
>  *I want to make love to you.*

Literally, *with* you. The shift is subtle.

I think about the last time he kissed me, *really* kissed me. I
think about thunderstorms, historic floods & wonder when
the fog will clear or the cumulus clouds will break up & finally
leave his leaden eyes. I think about the past & ask if we will
ever move away from there.

I hear the present is a nice place.

Some nights I can't sleep, so I catalogue him in the dark, bury
my face into his back & press lip to vertebrae. The heat of
pimiento rises languidly from clavicle, musky, like rain on
warm pavement. Zesty mandarin. Spicy accords of cardamom.

Pray that morning will be kind to us.

At the donut shop, indecision swirls in freshly poured cups of
coffee. He pulls me close & tries to decide which flavor he'd
like, or if he even wants to be with me. He speaks in L words;
I never know if the next will be I love you or I'm leaving you.
*I just love you,* he says.

We don't see our shadows that day.

# PEANUT BUTTER & MANIC SANDWICHES

This afternoon you called & asked where I was
because all you could hear was wind.

*I just jumped out of a plane,*
I said. *I'm skydiving.*

You found this funny, though you couldn't have known
by my tone how serious it was, having already fallen
through so many lithium clouds.

Later, while I was making peanut butter & manic sandwiches,
you wanted to know if I've been symptomatic.

*Well, I've been driving really fast,*
I said. *Warp speeds. You'll never catch me.*

You didn't have to ask what happened to my shoes.
I think you already knew I had no use for them
on my firecracker feet.

Not today, at least.

# BLOOD ORANGE & PLUM WASH

Burdens lifted. Blood orange
dripped from your chin. Night fled
in a plum wash above palm trees

fanning into dreamcatchers,
missing all the dreams.

You left Sunday
still sleeping in your bed,
curling slightly around the edges
of what was & could have been.

You kissed her on the forehead

& went.

# III. QUARTER

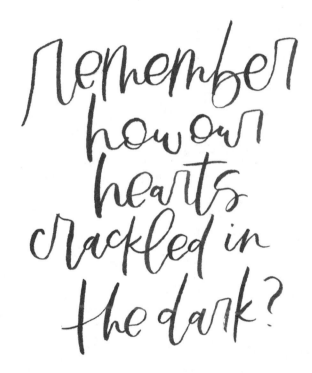

Remember how our hearts crackled in the dark?

Somewhere beneath this glass ceiling,
under canopies of LEDs & cosmic
string lights, you are breathing.

The thought alone levels cities
in my chest. I pin you beneath
the Tropic of Cancer—

a shuffle, misstep,
collapse & a kiss.

You have to know that I can't even look
at a Christmas tree without falling for you,
have to know that I still miss you on nights
so cold your name leaves my lungs in ghosts.

& if nothing else, you have to know,
I always hope it's warmer where you are.

## SLEEPING DRAGON

Maybe I wanted something easy, someone
who didn't ask the hard questions, just

"Does this feel good?" & "Is this okay?"

Yes. Yes. A thousand times yes.

Somewhere in the grove of your neck, cardamom
& orange blossom, lemon & pepper. Somewhere
in the hollow of your collarbone, a depression,
a hot breath blowing over sand dunes. Somewhere
unbuckling Adonis' belt, fingers like star trails,
telescope eyes adjusting to the light.
                    *Wide aperture, long exposure.*

Night is lifting in octagonal hues.
(Don't stop. Don't you dare stop.)

Ante meridian hours pass. You sneak out, careful
not to wake the sleeping dragon curling around
vowel sounds, still smoking, still swelling,
wings tucked between shoulder blades,
iridescent in the sheets. Beating.

                *Everything beating.*

"Babe, go back to sleep.
You look so good sleeping."

But there is a fire in my belly
& a world in need of burning.

# GENTLE WAKES, VIOLENT WAVES

I'm going to come inhabit
the space against your chest
& listen to your heartbeat
with stethoscope ears
& hum what I hear
under my breath.

"going under, going under,
never coming up"

Gentle wakes, violent waves,
I will love you either way.

Hold you while the fever breaks.
Hold you the whole way through.

"mayday mayday mayday"

I said that I will hold you.

## STRAWBERRY FIELDS & FADED FOREVERS

Sometimes you still wonder
what it would have been like
to love me.

Sometimes you blush sunsets, stay up
all night, moonlight spilling over
your lips, swallowing cities
by the spoonful, calcium quarries
crunching steel & concrete.

Sometimes we meet in dreams. We are
strawberry fields. We are faded
forevers, the missed breath of summer,
fire opal, watching cloud formations,
as predictable as weather patterns
& quantum mechanics.

& sometimes,
sometimes you still wonder,
don't you?

# THERE IS NOTHING TO SEE HERE

There is nothing to see here, just a lot of leg on a night too
cold to be showing some. A head full of stars & a handful of
question marks. A trumpet call at the back of the auditorium.
An aura, or maybe an omen, flickering rose gold, among other
inaudible hauntings.

I wonder if you know how beautiful you look in the shadows.
I brush your hair from your collarbone & bite your shoulder.
You laugh cherry back into your cheeks & we both break
character. But it's too late. Even the ghosts are blushing.

The rest is a fragmented blackout, a Giacomo Balla painting,
velocity, drinking & driving, the brass glare of streetlights,
some running fevers, all night blind.

> "You don't have to worry about me. I'm a
> professional."

> "I know. That's why I worry."

Hours from now, when my confidence has waned, when my
mane is matted to the back of my head, when I'm staring at
the mirror wondering who this stranger is, when I'm hating
myself more than the smell of juniper on the empty side of
the bed from men I've made love to but will never be in love
with, that is when I will write again. I'll use words like bright,
wildgrown, forest like.

I'll cut the bullshit & stick to what I'm good at—
picking poetry out of my teeth until my gums bleed.

## SPACE & SEA, YOU & ME

Romance was man exploring space
though he didn't know the sea.
It was wanting to discover you
when I still hadn't found me.

# THE TIME TRAVELER'S GUIDE TO PLANNING
# FUNERALS

"Tell me you don't want to be with me."

"What?"

"I said, tell me you don't want to be with me
& I'll leave right now."

"Don't do it like this."

---

This. Call it The Time Traveler's Guide to Planning Funerals.
Call it Exit Signs, Effervescent, Synaptic Failure. Call it All the
Things We Thought We Knew, or How to Lose Yourself in
Fractions. Call it words I should have written before you
stopped believing in the future—

the place where everything ends.

## OLD MAPS

How much must you
know of my past?
How will you find me
with old maps when
so many of my roads
are brand new?

# COURAGE & A COMPASS

*IN CASE OF EMERGENCY*
*BREAK THE GLASS*
*OF YOUR CHEST*

Find the following contents:

courage & a compass.

Maybe your heart's never given
the greatest directions,
but it's always done its best.

Listen to the ruckus,
the pound & the pulse.

*You've got this. You've got this.*

## TILTED HALO, CROOKED CROWN

When I grow up
I want to build empires
with my bare hands
just to knock them down

curtsy as they crumble
tilt my halo, crooked crown.

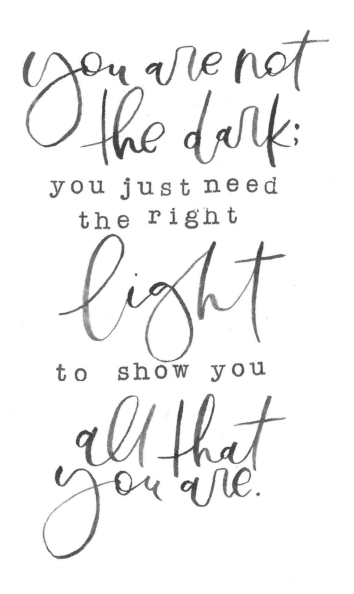

you are not
the dark;
you just need
the right
light
to show you
all that
you are.

# HOW TO TELL A STORM IS COMING

i.  Lick your fingertip. Hold it to the wind.
    Wait for Michelangelo to paint you into existence.
    Wait for Adam to find God. Witness frescoes
    dry    /    fade    /    peel.        When you feel
    you've waited long enough, wait some more.

ii. Understand this: prediction is not a religion.

iii. Fall down a rabbit hole. Now you're
     a cloud atlas, a weather pattern,
     mackerel skies & mares' tails,
     birds crowding power lines.

iv. Now I'm standing outside            watching
    stratus clouds              wondering
                    when the rain will come.

v.  Now my heart is a weathervane
    & the barometric pressure        of   my   blood
    is just enough to keep my wings tucked,
    to make me forget all I've ever known:

    shoulder blades & petrichor.

When I said
it comes in waves
I meant
that in the middle
of the clearest, calmest day
I see its hundred-foot face
in the distance—

the wall
barreling toward me.

Even if I survive
come out on the other side
there will always be
another Goliath
building
right behind it.

# FROM SPACE ALL OUR CITIES LOOK LIKE STARS

FROM EARTH
the moon looks like a small boat
drifting into obsidian. A black sea,
still as the day she left me.

I can't stand the sight of it.
        Caustic crescent.
                Waxing goddess.

So I set sail beyond the atmosphere
let the darkness decant
cozy up in spatial fabric
      with my favorite book.


FROM SPACE
she is not worth mentioning.


FROM SPACE
all our cities look like stars.

# THE TOPOGRAPHY OF YOUR BODY

i.   The weather makes my knees ache. I crumble
         into Epsom salt, tape paint
     samples to the sky & brainstorm ways to stay gray.

         Cinder block. Forged iron. Campfire smoke.

             Burnt ember. Pewter. Lava stone.

ii.  Poets should avoid eye contact & interviews.

         "What are your strengths?"

         "Vulnerability. Devouring people whole."

iii. Even now I can recall the topography of your body
         every inch soaked in opaline possibility
         every canyon, every curve luminesced.

     Even now I am surprised on the mornings I wake
     to find our bones still covered in flesh.

iv.  I want to be wide open. Vitreous. A house
         made of only windows.
     So transparent birds try to fly right through me.

## THE FERMATA

I grieve with my hands.

Fingers of a pianist,
long and delicate

like held breath.

I put them to work.
Scrub dishes,
      smooth sheets,
            pull weeds.

They stay busy.

By the end of the day
they curl under the weight;
my mind follows suit

& collapses into a heap.

A pile of magnolia leaves.
A pit of oak burned to ash.

I could write an entire book, call it
"Falling in Love at a Distance."
I could pack the pages with metaphors
about having tectonic plates for a rib cage,
how my heart rests on a fault line,
how it's no one's fault but mine.

I could write about imaginary lines
& states that shouldn't exist
simply because they come between us,
but that doesn't make any sense.

I won't write about that tonight.

Tonight I am dropping temperature,
low humidity, bracing for fall,
when my thoughts will dress up
like paper dolls & parade around
in layered rumination.

This is how the story ends.
(This is not how the story ends.)

# SONGS WITH OUR EYES CLOSED

FADE IN:

EXT. ATOP A SKYSCRAPER – NIGHT

Four legs dangle over the ledge of a high-rise. Below, light trails, halcyon from a distance, throwing gilded glints, carnelian meteors against the asphalt backdrop. Between laced fingers, neon. Two near-strangers sit, their shoulders squeezing empty space, trying to collapse the earth's lungs. A city, running out of breath, a symphony of horns and 'to hell with yous,' muted, spins its vinyl song.

> HER
> Just when you think you've made it through the worst, the universe delivers another blow. It's like we spend our whole lives learning how to navigate the pain. [pause] But there has to be more than this, right?

> HIM
> That's the thing. It hurts to exist.

A car crash in slow motion. Chopin's Nocturne in B-flat Minor, op. 9, no. 1 accompanies the accident. The impact is shown in fragments. Glass shatters. Metal folds. Airbags deploy.

Bleach. If you use enough bleach,
you can clean anything, even your
daydreams scaling rice terraces,
white travertine tiers gleaming
in the setting & forgetting.

I have not seen this shade of blue
since that day in Monteverde
when the taxi sputtered away in fumes
bought or borrowed from Kuwait
& left corneas looming in my irises,
had not seen it previously since Hume
asked me to imagine what was missing
& I couldn't until I met you.

Does that somehow still count?
            (They say I dreamt you up.)

Pamukkale, petrified waterfall—
I am so many frozen histories.
I am a hot spring of memories
of the men who dwell inside me;
they live like kings in cotton castles.

I just plan on melting away.

# SEISMIC ACTIVITY

At my funeral

I don't want anyone to speak
Over the absence of my voice

*No longer a cashmere static*

A voice poured like cold milk
Over a bowl of Rice Krispies

*No longer a crackling fire*

& when they lower my lifeless body
Into the ground, drop lilacs on my casket

I hope they think of me and tremble
Remember me hand-clutched-to-chest

Because of the aftershock & shake
When every word still aches

*No longer, no longer*

The very legacy of my work—

The kind of seismic activity
That makes passing strangers
Simultaneously stop & ask

*Did you feel that?*

This song is eight minutes & sixteen seconds long. A cathartic symphony of instrumental snowdrifts, wordless because what is there to say, except that you're gone.

You're gone.

& it's harder than I thought. *Your hand in mine. (Goodbye.)* But these are only lines. Science defines how it ends. A final flickering of the brain stem before the city inside your head goes dark.

I don't believe in science anymore. Give me legend & folklore. Tell me that north of here the electricity of her voice still hurtles into the earth at hundreds of miles per hour. That she exists in the pink—green—yellow—blue—violet collision of charged particles. The violent orange & white. That she dances on the nightside of the planet. Tell me the human spirit is inextinguishable. That her joy still sparkles on moonlit beaches in the Maldives, that her fire rages in forests across California, & that her synapses strike in Catatumbo lightning.

No, she is not gone. She has only passed on.

*& she is light. she is light. she is light.*

IV. CRESCENT

what more
can i say of

*your love?*

on my

*darkest nights*

it brings out the

*stars*

in me

What was the world before you?
A dull & aching gray, deadened
(with so many dead ends).
I can barely remember it.
But I will never forget the color
you birthed into the universe,
how the warm & cool of you
blended into heliotropic hues,
then emerged as twilight hours.
Everything I know about love
I learned the very first time
the moon shone on your skin,
that to me became lubricious,
& under lavender halos of light
I danced & romanced with you
& your glow-in-the-dark bones.

## INVINCIBLE

This morning when you rolled over
out of bed & left my embrace,
I did not fear for your safety.

Under covers of night I whispered
spells between your shoulder blades,
casting a shield over your body
with the imprints of my lips.

But you are not invincible—

you must come home before
the sun crashes into the earth
& shatters into a billion stars.

(You belong in my arms.)

I have a problem with NASA. They keep
taking pictures inside my brain & claiming it's outer space.
Don't believe me? Last week, Pandora's Cluster—
                    that was me watching sound waves,
bats echolocate, remembering what you said
about fumbling in the darkness for friendship.

We could learn a thing or two from bats, like
what happens when signals don't bounce back.

Don't get me started on the heart, or the supermassive
black hole discovered just last month. Now they're
                    studying the science of [falling out of] love.

On the event horizon, evergreen soldiers pantomime
the word pining. Nobody knows what they want.

Fables learned as children, now acted out as adults.

*The sky is falling! The sky is falling!*

Where is the boy crying wolf?

## HOLD STILL

This isn't the first time you've fallen
and I'm sure it won't be the last.
That's what happens when the body
grows faster than the man wearing it.

Even after all these years,
your skin feels like an oversized shirt
with too many pockets.

Hold still,
let me wipe the crumbs from your mouth,
garnet remnants of hearts you've consumed.
You didn't mean to, you said.
You were just hungry for something more
than what your stomach was built for.

Hold still,
let me blow the ash from your forehead,
from the creases lined by fires you've set.
When I asked why you were building
all these matchstick empires,
you said they were easier to burn.

Hold still,
let me grip your unhinged jaw
and kiss the existence out of you.

i.  I'm making a list of practical things:
    — always carry an umbrella
    — look both ways before crossing
    — don't fall in love during a monsoon,
       mid-summer, 2000 miles apart

ii. Here, in this garage, tattooing your
    whole body in anatomical hearts.

    It wasn't enough to wear love
    on your sleeve. See figure 3b.

         [It never was.]

iii. Fireworks. Between us, enough
     e l e c t r i c i t y  to light an entire city.

iv. What would Tesla think of our spark?

# HARBOR TOWNS

This town is different.

Six days ago we were strangers
smiling at each other from across the table.

His eyes were land. Mine were land—
locked. We were halfway home.

Somewhere in the harbor of my heart—

a ship dropped anchor.

On the surface he appears serene, glassy.
I want to know what storms rage inside of him,
what puts the wind in his sails, what makes him
the man he is. He asks where I've been.

*Waiting. Wading. Wait—*

suddenly
the shorelines of his lips
give way to oceans,

a depth I've never known.

# THE MARTIAN

Last summer I planned a road trip across your skin
but your face was    a mirage    a monolith    a melting clock
and somehow your name    dried up  got lost  in my voice box.

*Death Valley. Namib. The Atacama.*

What does it feel like to be an alien on your home planet?
            Something like excavating your own rib cage
                        (and calling it archaeology).
Tell me with a mouthful of red rock. Desert and dust.

How did you find me here? Give me coordinates.
What were    the chances    the odds    our paths would cross

            pointing satellites into empty space.

You and I, we live on the same wavelength.

Changing frequency --- adjusting antenna
            listening to the static in the dark
                        the charge and the spark
wondering if anyone else feels the way that I do
            and if      I'm standing at the edge of the earth

why does my heart look so much like Mars?

# TWO TRUTHS, ONE LIE

The kitchen table appears a continent and an arm's reach between us. We play two truths and one lie.

1. Some nights you stay awake counting stars. One for every regret. Two for every time you wished you were someone else.

2. You don't love me.

3. A black wolf visits you while you dream.

You never dream.

Tonight I am missing you in spectrums. Ultraviolet light, the
clear of coconut rum. Sun-soaked skin, the color of burnt
umber, mushroom and mud. Tonight I am losing you in hues.
The way the blue of the mountains fades the farther away they
are. The way a cooling star goes red before it burns out.
Sometimes I think about dimensions, and how if I stand in
the doorway where we said goodbye, we are still together in
every dimension but time. I put my hand to the bodiless space
where your cheek would be and tell you I love you. Invisible
you. So close, so impossibly far.

# DANDELION CLOCKS

One day we will talk about
how our blue moon wish came true.
How, when the universe finally released
the pins that held us so remote,
we did not fall, suddenly and all at once,
but rather drifted toward each other
with the whimsical grace
of dandelion clocks.

grief is the name we give to the ghosts of those we have lost

# SINGULARITIES

There must have been a breakdown of space and time the night you died. A singular point. A collapsing of your soul into something else. Into someplace else. Sometimes I write out loud. What is the word for the way tail and traffic lights reflect on wet pavement? Reds and yellows and greens, all blurry bright. The way the inky black of the road holds the glow. Sometimes I swear I see your face in a stranger's face. In the lips, the jaw, the eyes. What I mean is I have seen the world glitch in broad daylight. I invent new theories to account for the vanishings. If supermassive black holes exist, then why can't the opposite? Consider that a microscopic singularity has occurred in my brain, is devouring cells, neurons, intercepting moments, destroying memories. Maybe if I write enough fiction, the rules and laws of relativity and nature and mourning will no longer apply and I won't have to accept what I am so afraid to accept:

that I am simply forgetting.

as if we are
in the backyard lounging
on Adirondack chairs
      looking up
tell me the center of our galaxy
smells like raspberries
and tastes like rum
that somewhere beyond the dust
cloud of Sagittarius B2 a harmonica wails
                              a guitar strums
hold your doomsday baton
conduct the insects
a cacophony of crickets
and winged instruments
      crescendo
cue the light show above
a brilliant display of dynamite
all  b o o m  and  P O P
barbeque a thousand suns
the way astronauts describe outer space
as metallic, sweet-smelling
as gunpowder and burned steak
      make a metaphor
how like summer
we whimper     out of existence
      sizzle. singe. evaporate.

# SLOW DRAG

## I.

The Time Traveler, a native, stands watch over Pack Square,
dons a military jacket and fingerless gloves. Asheville,
     then and now.   Now and then
     he flickers    in and out    of existence
smoking unfiltered cigarettes
writing a poem, "How to Hold a Moment in Your Lungs."

## II.

Maybe it's in our blood: juniper berries, pine needles, acorn.
Maybe there's a verse
               for how we found ourselves
                       on the forest floor.

## III.

Mark the elevation

remark how the world looked    a lot smaller
when you were standing       five thousand feet
                      above
                    it all.

and slingshot like a comet. Park on the astral overlook. Gaze across the black of space and twinkling string lights. Call this city a galaxy. Talk about life, the universe, and everything. Kiss until the stars go out. Find every excuse to not go home, or back to earth, and stay here in this moment. This one breathless moment. This place where yours and mine converge and these become *our* lips *our* limbs *our* words.

Let's colonize the night.

Here, *right here*. This could work.

# A LOVE LIKE MINE

Because your light
is not quite like mine.

Your grays are not
gray like mine.

But your wants
could be met in time,

should you want
a love like mine.

I'm thirty years old. Don't ask me how it happened. I blink and ten years pass. I take a breath and forget. I forget to take a breath.

I'm thirty years old and what that means is I've lived a third of my life without you. What's a decade? Ten years and two fists and not a fight left in me.

Perhaps I have become unstuck. In time. In space. In mind.

Did you ever read Vonnegut? Another question I'll never get to ask. According to the Tralfamadorians you did not die, only appeared to die, and are very much still alive in the past. How tender, how romantic. The past always has and always will exist. You and I are simply trapped in different ambers, different moments. All we have to do is change tense.

Last night I dreamt of teeth churned onto the beach from storm surge. Their dull points. Their fossilized roots. The slate and mud of their color. In some continuum they are still intact. White and gnashing. Today the winds howled and the hurricane rained. Today I did not leave my room. Instead, I stood in the stormy glow from my window and photographed my abdomen. I thought about the navel / umbilicus / belly button.

This cavern. This scar. This mark left by the woman I once belonged to.

This hole in the very center of me.

## PHILIPPIANS 2:14-15

Who am I kidding? We'll never be blameless.

But maybe if we're compassionate,
if we praise more and complain less,
maybe if we're generous,
if we give more and take less,
maybe if we're altruists, virtuous,
if we practice kindness, evolve,
master our own faults, our own flaws,
recognize the difference
between stars and singularities,
become stelliferous,
maybe learn to be nocturnal,
maybe see through all this darkness,

maybe then,
we can be forgiven.

Maybe then,
we can shine brighter than the rest.

# HIRAETH

A home which never was.

The shutters
On our first home
Were blue
In a parallel universe
We keep the baby
His birthday cake decorated
With trick candles
Blow.blow.blow
See how his lungs draw
Smokeless breath
A wish come true
He just turned seven
And I don't have to wonder
What we named him

# THE HORIZON IS NOT A LINE

When you can't sleep, you tell yourself creation stories. Crack the cosmic egg on the back of a giant tortoise. Dream your druzy dreams. The world is a boundless ocean. Without shore, without horizon. You drift there, in a time before time, cerulean in every direction, glinting under invisible suns. *Bad astronomy*, you think, and sink below the surface. Dissolve into molecules. Become aqueous. Let the primeval sea swallow you up.

I've been asking too many questions lately
        like how are you today?
        and were most of your stars out?
        and do you love me?

                *You don't have to answer that.*

I've been reading about polyphasic sleep
        Leonardo da Vinci
        Edison and Tesla

I worry I am not awake enough
        not creating enough
        not (in)sane enough

My friend says I worry too much.

He says we are helium.
Never as heavy as we seem.

The only place left to go
is up.

v. **NEW**

There's nothing more
to the story.

When we met
he looked like forever
& I swore I'd love him
slow as summer.

It's been August
ever since.

# THE WRAITH

## I.

On the morning the news breaks the front yard is a blanket of
birds and nobody knows the word for this. Everyone sits in
the living room, mouths moving inaudibly like a television on
mute. In the afternoon we compare the composition of our
tears on microscope slides. We cry so hard we laugh; we laugh
so hard we cry. There is a chemistry to our sadness and it all
comes down to salt.

## II.

Two days after you pass I drive by Boeing and imagine a hole
in the assembly line. I wonder if anyone can read blueprints
for a world in which you do not exist. I contemplate the
mechanics of flight and consider how my bones have been
hollowed by a life so full of loss. Airplanes break apart and fall
from the sky.

## III.

Three days and you have not yet risen. The moon orders a
memorial but the tide does not listen. The bay brims with
white paint. On this long road to the sea, a small fishing boat
gets a makeover. Four red handprints, two fatherless sons. In
blue letters: You should be here.

## IV.

On the fourth day I cross the intersection where the accident
happened and see roses tied to the telephone pole. The wreck
has been cleared, but the pain is still everywhere. You can feel
it hanging in the air, tugging on traffic lights. Lingering in the
median—a wraith.

## V.

Five days have gone by. Five. I count them on grieving fingers.

## VI.

Day six, we bury you in the earth. Corpses and calla lilies. I wonder how many others cram into the casket. Parts of us only known by you. Secrets between friends, family, lovers. Perhaps we should hold funerals for ourselves too.

## VII.

Seven days and I still have an ache in my side. I dig into my abdomen to find your rib stuck between my ribs; it is the way God created women.

And like this I will carry you with me.

# LITTLE LION, ROAMING THE COLD GOLDEN

I don't need a photograph to remember.
Loving you has been a series of moments.
(In this moment, you're saving my life.)

That winter brought ice
                    downed power lines
                    rolling blackouts.

Think weather as metaphor.
            Imagine a sadness that stretches for miles.
                    The future frozen over.

Were we to overwinter, I wonder,
what season would we become?

You smile,
and the ground begins to thaw.

You laugh,
and the world stops just to watch the melt.

You run wildly towards a dying sun.
Oh, how you lean into the light.

The site of the last supper.
Where I go to be with your ghost.

No one ever said if you were drinking that night, but I hope
you were. Hope you were all bowed strings and burning
tempo. Accordion and trilled r's. An ensemble of smooth
vocals and brass horn. Polka rhythm and acoustic guitar.
Hope when you left your friends and revved your brand-new
motorbike right onto Rivers, veins aflood with tequila and
triple sec, fresh-squeezed orange and lime, that you were
under the influence of the night. All endorphin, no fear.
Feeling invincible, though you never were. Hope you were
buzzed when you pummeled into the van crossing onto
Dunlap with so much force you overturned it. Hope God
plucked your soul from your body long before it ever hit the
ground. 250.feet.away. Where you lay. And lay. And lay.
Where paramedics found you, a mangle of flesh and bone and
fabric and blood. Where you were identified by your wife's
name tattooed on the nape of your neck. Where it was
somebody's job to pronounce you dead.

No one ever said if you were drinking that night, but I hope
you were. Hope you never felt a thing, or what I'm feeling
now. This sour stomach. This belly-churning emptiness.

*This death. This death.*

## LUCKY NUMBERS

I'm running out of lucky numbers; I'm running out of luck. It's been seven years since I rested my head against your sinking chest, begging idle tides to put the moon back in the sky again. Seven years since you held me in the doorway, arms draped around my shoulders, a cloak I wish I could carry with me always. That was the last time I saw you.

Sometimes I think I didn't hold you long enough.

Lately I've been praying to my own hands because you told me God lives in them. I've been painting my nails oxblood and worshipping the words my fingers pen. Maybe if I create enough beautiful things, I'll be able to find you in them.

When I bought my first home, I surrounded it in black holes, because land mines weren't enough to keep your ghost away. You still came knocking at my door.

Every time I finish weeding my heart, I have to begin again. Missing you is unlike any labor I've ever known. Even when I feel bloodless and my split-chambered heart pumps nothing but question marks through collapsing veins and salt water fills my lungs, I hear you telling me that I'm enough. And now my abdomen is a patchwork of wire mesh from all the times I've tried to keep from spilling my guts.

The truth is, the days between get easier but the anniversaries hurt worse. I feel guilty for the days I don't mourn your passing, for days I'm not the woman I want to be, a daughter you could be proud of.

I'm still trying to be enough.

## MULTIVERSE

what wicked tragedy
what cruel cosmic trick

that there should exist a universe
in which you and I are together
                . . . and this is not it.

# I'VE KEPT QUIET FOR SO LONG

when I open my mouth
I'm frightened by the sound
of my own voice.

More salt than syrup.
More rocket launch than crackling fire.

# APEX PREDATOR

   i.    THE WOLF MOON RISES

behind power lines; she is a promise
ring of precious metal. The sky, morganite,
splinters black branches of barren trees
diverting into dusty rose like bronchioles.
Night, now a collapsed lung, grabs us by our fur
coats. We stumble into the champagne dark.
            We curse the stars.
              Curse the soot-covered sidewalks
illuminated by street lamps, forgotten by gods.


   ii.    WINTER DOES NOT COME—

I hold my breath.
I am the hunter and the hunted.

January bangs the brass at my doorstep.
           *Nobody's home. Nobody's home.*


   iii.    I DON'T KNOW HOW TO WRITE A POEM

that doesn't start or end with my body,
don't know how to put pen to paper
without giving birth

         to      the howl and the hunger
                 the hell and the hurt.


   iv.    MY HEART IS AN APEX PREDATOR;

it always goes for the throat.

Sometimes I
find mementos
of who I used to be
a thousand women ago
    *-the scar below my lip*
    *-freckles on the tip of my nose*

Sometimes I
right myself through dreamlike
dimension. delusion.

    *I flutter. I float.*

Sometimes I
catch a glimmer
catch a glimpse
    of a girl
    of a ghost

# STANDING ON SUNKEN CITIES

"Sleep in as long as you'd like. The aspirin is in the kitchen."

Did he kiss my head when he left? I don't remember.
Did we use protection? I don't remember that either.

The secret to surviving hangovers: a hot shower.
Expanding blood vessels allow more oxygen to the brain,
relieving tension until painkillers kick in.          I open
cabinets, push aside niacin and protein powder.          I think
of him, the shape of him, barrel-chested and brawny,
how his skin smells of citrus and mahogany.

In the bathroom, a naked window looks into the woods.
Sunlight darts past bicep and breast, flittering wingless;
                              *where is the poetry in this?*

Sleeping with married men. Standing on sunken cities.

I feel faint, travel to a stream, hear trickling, surface slaps.
Back in the shower, I turn the faucet higher while my
thoughts return to my own burning body, stand there until I
am speckled, gray in places, until I am salmon-colored,

dignity sloughing off like the skin of some dead fish.

things i learned
from the

moon:
at times you
may feel like
a sliver of
yourself.
there is
beauty
in this
too.

# I AM LOOKING FOR MY MOTHER

Have you seen her?
I wake from dreams where she walks the earth, breathless, her
name cotton on my tongue. Every thin floral fragrance could
lead me straight to her. I turn my head when top notes of
orange and lily stand out in crowds of nameless faces.
Sometimes I visit plantation gardens or florists searching for
violet, jasmine, Egyptian tuberose. Other times I comb the
woods for earthy scents of oak moss and sandalwood. In my
closet dwell piles of old clothes soaked in elegant vintage
nuance. I cover my face in her ammonia and breathe sorrow
deep into my being. I drive by her house but a new mother
lives there now, with new children who do not look like my
sisters or me. When I meet her again in dream I ask where she
has been. *Trying to find you*, she says. In waking life I know this
to be impossible. Against all rationality I search because it is
the only act that brings me peace and where I find purpose,
that temporarily fills the unfillable hole left in my soul from
her departure, a search I cannot abandon until my own days
are numbered and I am nothing but a pile of bones born of
her bones.

I am looking for my mother.
Have you seen her?

*The pills were round. They called them orange, but they were more of a peach than anything, a color trying too hard to look like flesh, to insinuate living.*

In Avalon, a ghost bicycles around 29<sup>th</sup> Street on a classic red frame, coming & going impossibly slow. Whenever the service bell rings at the Sunoco, I know it's him. I feel better if I don't look.

*25mg was a small dose. That's why I took so many.*

When the island's outdoor warning system sounds,
     I am lucid
     I am moving my vehicle to higher ground
     I am cracked wind
vacuuming ash from the third-story balcony
my veins are pumping gasoline.

*Everything has side effects, if you think about it.*

I don't know who I am without the people I love. Am I losing them all to floods? They rot; we rust. We put them to rest.

*The side effect of living is death.*

# MIDAS TOUCHED THE MOUNTAINS

the        blue ridge        turned golden
below                the escarpment
        the vermillion and gilt
of rusted car frames   and   all the hearts
that had been stolen
        that night
we   spray – painted  the stars
graffitied                over     bald rock
shared     a          single pillow
on a        blow – up          mattress
                our limbs   *made of metal*
    our tongues   *tasting iron*
and I                wondered
if we had                the same dream.

# PROPHECY

It happened just like you said:

THE OCEAN SWALLOWED THE CITY

barreled in like a plague
drowned every street
in love & lunacy

& when it came to an end
I could no longer remember
which I had been

the poison or the tonic
the metropolis or the sea

# WHAT IS SHE?

What mile were you on when you
stopped to admire the long-stemmed
roses strewn about the beach?
How long were you standing there
that the tide came in & circled
your ankles, sunk your feet?
Was it then that you wondered,
*What is she?* The sand or the sea.
The bone white of those petals,
the ocean foam, the way every
coastal city feels like home.
When you begged your legs to leave
they asked, *What for? She's the
reason we won't run anymore.*

## OR MAYBE I AM THE MOON

My only purpose—
to make the tides
rise & fall
in you.

## NON-EXHUMABLE

There are some things we don't talk about, memories sealed in tiny metal coffins marked "non-exhumable." We cut the utilities, board up the windows of our hearts, condemn the whole goddamn structure.

I was with my father when he got the phone call that you kissed the creator goodnight for the last time. I saw his face so wet with pain I could have hydroplaned over his eyes.

My father doesn't cry.

I've moved on from asking why because I've been through this enough times to know by now that it's the one question I'll never have an answer to. But maybe you can help me with these:

Where did your soul go the night it fled from the war-torn country of your body like a refugee?

When will my father give up the guilt he's been coveting? The ghosts? The "Get Out of Jail Frees?"

How do I bury you six feet in my frame when I only stand 5'9"?

# A FOOTNOTE ABOUT HOPE[1]

---

[1] And how it holds us, still    it holds us    still, it holds.

# THE SUMMER I OUTLIVED SYLVIA

was a swarm of bees      a droning in my throat
a poem I could not purge      so I swallowed the sting.

June was an oven stuck on preheat, did not come with
instructions. Straggler cicadas emerged, snapping their wings.
Who welcomed them? A woman with two heads, a month
pregnant with neglect. Ruby-bellied fruit fell from their stems;
the strawberry moon overripened.

July softened into mud. Foundations sunk. Death came to our
own backyard to claim the operator of one riding lawnmower
sputtering around the lake, which slid down the embankment
and flipped, pinning man beneath machine. He drowned in
broad daylight. The neighbors buzzed around outside.

August brought its own miseries. We discovered widows
nesting in the back room, forgot how to make a metaphor,
could not look at a surface without also considering its
rupturing. Even the ocean's skin, darkly glittering, was just
that, skin. Something you could pierce or shed. You never
knew what would slash through that blue impasto, that knifed
gloss. A leviathan. A body. A fin.

By September there was only the gash in the earth, a mason
jar full of larva shells, the random silken sandspur—tokens of
those halcyon hauntings.

The summer I outlived Sylvia

was all rain and death      a thunderstorm quivering cobwebs
each lightning bolt an execution      flashing against the wet
wad of words      an egg sac      a swollen hourglass

of venom      of honey      of wing.

## OCTOBER COMES

& I am the pale-yellow husk
of the person I once was.

# GRATITUDE

For you, dear reader.
For giving my words a home.

# INDEX